T0063156

BASKETBALL
Visionetics

MENTAL
PREPARATION
FOR BETTER PLAY

EDWIN L. ATLAS

Masters degree Education
Additional Study: Certificate of Sports Hypnotherapy

AAU coach, US Army player/coach

BALBOA
PRESS
A DIVISION OF HAY HOUSE

Balboa Press books may be ordered through booksellers or by contacting:

Balboa Press
A Division of Hay House
1663 Liberty Drive
Bloomington, IN 47403
www.balboapress.com
1 (877) 407-4847

Because of the dynamic nature of the Internet, any web addresses or
links contained in this book may have changed since publication and
may no longer be valid. The views expressed in this work are solely those
of the author and do not necessarily reflect the views of the publisher,
and the publisher hereby disclaims any responsibility for them.

The author of this book does not dispense medical advice or prescribe
the use of any technique as a form of treatment for physical, emotional,
or medical problems without the advice of a physician, either directly
or indirectly. The intent of the author is only to offer information
of a general nature to help you in your quest for emotional and
spiritual well-being. In the event you use any of the information in
this book for yourself, which is your constitutional right, the author
and the publisher assume no responsibility for your actions.

Any people depicted in stock imagery provided by Thinkstock are
models, and such images are being used for illustrative purposes only.
Certain stock imagery © Thinkstock.

Printed in the United States of America.

ISBN: 978-1-4525-8705-9 (sc)
ISBN: 978-1-4525-8704-2 (e)

Balboa Press rev. date: 4/1/2014

Contents

Dedication

To basketball players at all levels looking
for the empowering mental edge

Author's Note: Basketball Visionetics is a
collection of mental lyrical poems for all ages
and for both genders. For easier reading
comprehension, I wrote using
the male pronoun throughout the
text. As you continue reading
you will discover that I use the pronoun
"he" instead of "he/she."
This is done only to simplify the reading.

Epigraph

The general who wins a battle makes many calculations
in his temple before the battle is fought. – Sun Tzu

Basketball Visionetics Introduction

Basketball Visionetics is a collection of motivational
poems that are visual, audio, and kinesthetic.

The poems include questions and other mental
cues for basketball players to learn and use.

For example: What do you do when
you take a shot and badly miss?
Do you get upset in a negative response to this?

How do you get out of a shooting slump?
How about when you're so tired you think you can't jump?

There are notes on how to overcome losing
and pre-game mantras for your choosing.

Some poems will push players to fight
harder as they play to win
and motivate them to never give up
through thick and thin.

There are tips to help ballers eliminate bad mental habits and play better basketball under pressure and handle stress. There are techniques that enable them to transform their energies into positive game-changing success empowering them to play in the zone with superior court consciousness.

Are you a player?

Do you play basketball or are you a basketball player?

Which one of the above two, defines and describes you?

This may seem confusing to some, but it's not a riddle.
You are one or the other, there is no middle.

Do you eat, drink, dream, sleep, and live for basketball?
Or would you rather hang with friends in
the video arcade at the shopping mall?

Would you go to the gym early in the
morning or late at night?
Or would you only shoot hoops
when the time seems right?

Are you born to ball? Is it in your genes?
If you are a baller, then you know what it means.

You don't take time off at the end of the season.
You just want to ball for a purpose, a goal and a reason.

The game means more to a baller than one who just plays.
If you ask a baller why, they can count the ways.

Baller's go hard to better their game,
With passion and heart burning like a flame.

They love to ball and always play their best.
They want to get to the next level in every conquest.

He/she who just plays whenever and just plays for the fun,
is the type who does not want to work-out or run.

There is a difference in the hunger level between the two.
The baller can't go without balling and
wouldn't know what to do.

While the type who just plays basketball
could take or leave it,
The player finds a way to get to a
court. You better believe it!

That's the type of player that coaches are looking for.
They want basketball players who want it more.

If you are a basketball player, then you set the bar high.
You will play every game all out like it's do or die.

Always keep focused and reach for your goal.
Always play your heart out with all of your soul.

Believe!

Believe in yourself, in your shot.
Believe you can score
from any spot on the floor.

Believe in your coach,
Believe in your team.

Believe you can achieve
whatever you dream.

Believe in hard work to build physical and mental muscle,
Believe you can make game winning
plays as you always hustle.

Believe you hold your own against any player you guard.
Believe there is no challenge is too
difficult, no challenge too hard.

Believe you are un-guardable and can't be stopped.
Believe your work ethic and desire can't be topped.

Believe you will win every time that you play.
Believe you will bring the fire each and every day.

Believe you can get better and challenge yourself to excel.
Believe you can always improve and
always expect to do well.

Believe you can when you think you can't.
Believe in yourself is a mental seed you must plant.

Believe the seed will grow and blossom just like a flower.
Remind yourself to believe at least once an hour.

Believe you can comeback from any setback.
Never give up and never give yourself any slack.

If you doubt yourself, go harder and even fake it.
Believe in yourself like you know will make it.

Keep believing in yourself like a song
playing on continuous repeat.
Playing over and over, shake your head and pat your feet.

Snap your fingers and clap your hands.
Remind yourself to believe by wearing wrist rubber bands.

Believe no matter what the naysayers say.
Always believe where there's a will, there's a way.

Keep believing no matter what the rhyme or reason.
Keep believing all year around even during off-season.

G.S.3 (Game Shots, Game Spots, Game Speeds)

The best workout practice any baller needs
is to take and make GAME SHOTS, from
GAME SPOTS, at GAME SPEEDS!!!

Work on shots you know you can consistently make.
Shots that in game situations you would normally take.

Don't waste time shooting shots that are
out of your range or position.
Practice shooting good shots that you
will take against real competition.

Always start shooting from the close range inside
spots, find your stroke and get in a groove.
Then, when you feel comfortable making
shots you can step out and move.

Knock down a least 5 consecutive shots
from one spot and make it rain.
Shoot hundreds of shots, feel no pain, no gain.

Take shots off the dribble and shots off the pass.
Take shots off a screen, and shots off the glass.

Make shots with contact and a hand in your face.
Make shots wide open and shots with
little or no room or space.

Use the seven main spots on the half court floor:
Left and right wings, elbows, the corners
and from the top of the key to score.

Challenge yourself to make at least one hundred shots
from each of those seven scoring spots.

Practice shooting with purpose and a set goal in sight.
The homework you do will help to
get your game just right.

Strive to beat yourself and raise the bar.
If you make this your daily routine it will take you far.

If you practice hundreds of repetitions
whenever you train,
your muscle memory will be stored in your brain.

Keep it simple and always go as hard as you can.
He who works hardest will be the last standing man.

Go hard even when you think you don't have the strength.
Go from your gut and take it to the next length!

Go one more round, get up one more shot,
leave it on the floor and give it all you've got.

No matter how many shots it takes,
finish your practice session with three straight shot makes.

That's money deposited in your memory bank
with compound interest in your shooting tank.

Game-Face

Game-face is a state of mind
If you look within yourself you will find.
You can relax yourself and just unwind
to play on a higher level of another kind.

You play with passion, purpose and in the zone.
Game-face helps you play with a mellow tone.

Strike at the defense's gaps with
sharp cuts and crisp passes.
Attack whenever the defense is relaxed
and knock them on their masses.

Don't let any team know how to prepare.
Look them dead in their eyes with a "game-face" stare.

Catch them off guard; go explosive and hard.
Always go the extra yard and make it your calling card.

Always keep your plans of attack unknown.
Play without your trump card being shown.

Step on the court with a focused poker game-face,
to show you are ready to ball, anytime, anyplace.

Spin off every block, bump, pick or screen.
Square up for every shot on balance,
with your game-face gleam, keen-eyed and mean.

Keep your game simple as one, two and three.
Always have a move A, a counter-move B,
and the Counter-to-the-counter move C.

Are you ready to shoot when you catch the ball?
Do you over react when you get a bad call?

Do you know when to go fast and when to slow it down?
Can you play when you are angry and without a frown?

Do you pout whenever things don't turn out right?
Do you think about your game in your sleep at night?

You can control your mind over matter,
if you learn to shut out and erase the external chatter.

Do you handle the pressure; can you take a hard foul?
Can you blow that dust off your
shoulder and simply smile?

Do you make something happen on every play?
Can you never let obstacles get in your way?

Do you keep your game-face focus thru thick and thin?
Can you play all out with the mental
toughness and will to win?

Play the game within your head and maintain a game-face.
Always ready and steady no matter what the score or pace.

Play under pressure, in control and never sweat.
Your game-face will help you to never worry or fret.

Rock your game-face in every battle,
through thick and thin.
Always wear your game-face whether you lose or win.

Pre-Game Prep

Get your game-face with a pre-game pump
To prepare yourself for any game bump.

Use the following basketball mental "visionetics"
As a warm up with audiovisual kinesthetics.

These are motivating and empowering lyrical drills,
to unleash and explode your basketball skills.

If you feel anxious, nervous or a little queasy,
Relax with slow deep breathing and take it easy.

Shake your arms and legs, even
wiggle your fingers and toes.
Inhale through your mouth and exhale from your nose.

Get your game face glaze and radiate
a transcendental tone.
It makes you ready to play with harmony
and rhythm locked in the zone

As you put on your socks and tighten up your shoes,
silently repeat to yourself the following mental queues.

This is my pre-game ritual preparation
and I am tightening my focus and concentration.

I use my favorite music and listen to the rhythm and tone,
using the beat to get relaxed and into the zone.

While I stretch my body I stretch my imagination,
to tap into my powers of creative visualization.

I tap myself three (3) times on my heart and
head, also I tap the floor with my feet.
This is a code to remind myself to play
my best game and always compete.

I practice the same way every time I
step on a court or go to the gym.
As I step onto the court I lock my eyes on the
backboard and I center my attention on the rim.

I size up the basket from both sides, then
from the bottom up to the top.
As I see the square and the goal get bigger
and I can see my shots drop.

I focus my eyes and zero in on the
basket like a laser beam.
As I also use peripheral vision to see my whole team.

I lock in my mind to play with purpose
and get in a team players groove.
I always know when or where to be on the
court and the right time to move.

Basketball Jones

You can use music with lyrics and beats to
mentally help you play in the "Zone".
It can ignite the basketball jones oozing
thru your muscles and bones.
Study these words of hoop wisdom to
create positive vibrations and tones.

Every time you get ready to play your game,
Your pre game preparation needs to be the same.

Keep a simple and relaxing mental routine,
Remove any distractions and wipe your slate clean.

Find your favorite slow jam and beat to get
your mind and body in the groove.
Use music that makes you feel like you want
to just get on the dance floor and move.

Choose a short mantra and repeat the line
over the rhythm of the musical beat.
Let it resonate in your body, from your head and
shoulders, all the way down to your feet.

Say to yourself, "I am winner and I know I've got game"!
Imagine the announcer calling out your name.

Keep that fired up feeling steadily flowing and growing
Let the fire in that flame keep readily glowing.

Buzzer beaters

How do you get prepared and focused
for a game winning shot?
Can you get your shot off quickly from any spot?

Do you read the defense and use
the space that you've got?
If you have rehearsed this mentally
before then defense matters not.

When you catch the ball just relax and let it go.
You're in the zone and you can feel the flow.

You are confident and act just like you know.
You can count the basket as sure and
pure; it's automatic, it's good to go.

Stay focused on the rim and hold your follow thru.
Keep your eyes locked on the rim like you know it's true.

Silence defenders or the crowd noise and chatter.
That's your harness of the mental
power of mind over matter.

Anger Management

When the going gets tough, you must know what to do.
You can't give in to your anger, and
let it ruin the game for you.
Keep your head stay in the game. Chill
and keep your anger tame.
Inhale, relax and let it flow. Exhale
and let your game face show.
Don't explode or loose your cool. Don't
make yourself look like a fool.
Stay focused and always be a threat.
Never let them see you sweat.
Every time you step on the court. Bring
your "A" game to this sport.
Play hard through tough times, thick and thin.
You hate to lose more than you like to win.
Think of your team and see the big S.T.A.R.*

(Stop* Think* Act* Remember*)

The light beams on you wherever you are.
STOP*: take 3 deep breaths, and then count to
ten. Say to yourself I am a STAR, I play to win.
THINK*: and decide what do I chose. If I
fight my team and I automatically lose.
ACT*: Walk away to a better day and I will still be able to play.
REMEMBER*: What it takes to be a STAR,
is to be greater than you already are.
Don't get baited by players taunting, it can lead to
danger. It will take you out of the game if you
can't control and transform your anger.

You can brush it off your shoulder to stay in
the game and play even better and bolder. Stay
calm, chill, cool as ice and even colder.
Nothing can stop you when you play in the zone. No
person can break you with a stick, words or stone.
Ignore the crowd when you play in enemy gym
terrain. Just inhale, exhale and relax your brain.
Learn to be patient and always humble. Learn
not to complain, hold a grudge or grumble.

Always think before you talk. Always
be aware before you walk.

Give every person a firm handshake. Don't
sweat it whenever you make a mistake.

Just shake it off and let it go. Don't give
a bad seed the time to grow.

Keep your head up in spite of the score. You
are still a winner to the bone and core.

Maintain your composure and just be cool; on
the court, at home and also in school.

It doesn't matter about your size or height. What
counts is if you are ready and fit to fight.

Not with your fists but with your basketball game.
That's how your let them know your name.

How to Get over the Hump and Out of any Slump!

When most players miss a shot or make mistakes,
they hear the questions their inner mental judge makes.

This judge doesn't help the player's
confidence or correct the situation.
It just starts a snowball effect of more
confusion and frustration.

When it rains it pours is what they used to say.
Miss one shot, then another and it
affects the way they play.

They stop taking shots and give up on defense.
Now they can't figure out what's wrong;
it doesn't make any sense.

The problem is caused by their subconscious mind,
whispering judgmental comments at any fault it can find.

Why can I hit the open shot?
How come I can't get my game hot?

What's wrong with my form, why can't I shoot right?
Why can't I do anything good tonight?

I was fouled and the ref didn't make the call?
Why can't I even catch the ball?

I am so nervous and I don't know why?
I can't hit a jump shot no matter
what I do or how hard I try.

I don't know what to do about my shooting slump.
Why can't I get higher elevation on my jump?

Why am I playing so tense and tight?
Why I am feeling like I just want to fight?

Why are the coach and my teammates
always yelling at me?
Why don't my teammates pass me the
ball when I am open and free?

Why won't they feed me the ball when I just hit a three?
Why can't I get a call from that referee?

How come every turnover is my fault or bad?
Why can I play well like the last good game I had?

How come my shots don't even make
it up and over the rim?
Why am I shooting enough bricks
to build a brand new gym?

Why are other players always talking
trash my around my way?
Why does it get me so mad that I can't even play?

This is just a sample of judging questions you may hear.
Breaking your game-face down until it
becomes distracted and unclear.

A simple strategy you can use is to delete the negative
questions with constructive positive queues.
Here are a few questions to help to think
of better solutions you can choose.

What just happened? What are the facts?
Take a second to breathe, rewind, review and relax.

What are you thinking, feeling or wanting?
What's possible? How can I get out of
this slump that is haunting?

Choose a question and keep asking
yourself for 21 consecutive days.
Ask yourself mentally to help improve
your game in positive ways.

Why am I a great team player in every game?
How can I keep my negative demons tame?

Why do I make the right game decision?
Why do I play tough and use my peripheral vision?

Why do I have great concentration?
Why I play with heart and determination?

Why do I have great focus? Why do
I have great court sense?
Why do I have great footwork? Why
do I play tenacious defense?

Why do I have a knack for the ball?
Why I always play big and tall?

Why am I a great passer? Why am I a great cutter?
Why is my jumper smooth and pure as butter?

Why am I a great ball handler and such a clutch shooter?
Why do I play basketball like a game computer?

Why am I a great faker, risk taker,
a solid finisher and big shot taker?

Why am I am great defender?
Why am I a great help sender?

Why am I a renegade relentless rebounder?
Why does my game always grow to
be fundamentally sounder?

How can I quickly use synergy to get
over any setbacks or slumps?
How can I use my energy and bounce back
from any obstacles, hurdles or bumps?

Got Benched?

When the buzzer sounds and your
teammate calls out your name,
Do you think to yourself, why did
coach take me out of the game?

I was just getting started! I need more playing time!
I feel like I was a robbery victim of a horrible crime!

How do you handle the substitution
and sentence to sit on the pine?
Do you suck your teeth, poke out your
lip, roll your eyes and whine?

Or do you take the time to analyze
what you did right or wrong.
Do you take it in stride and be a team
player striving to get along?

Take time to get some water or a sports drink
As you allow your video mind to
replay, analyze and think.

Watching the game from a sideline view,
can trigger new ideas and insight
into what you can also do.

Look for weaknesses, gaps or breakdowns
as you search for flaws.
Seek new solutions that can change the effect and cause.

Use the bench time to add fuel to your fire.
Turn your anger into energy and positive desire.

Repeat to yourself your favorite
basketball affirmations or cues
While you take time to regroup and re-tie your shoes.

Get a grip on your game and find
your focus to play in the zone.
Bounce back and play to win with a positive tone.

Leave the last play behind, forgive
yourself and just let it go.
Catch the new wave of energy and
ride with the positive flow.

Listen to your coaches when they criticize your game
Own up to your mistakes and simply take the blame.

Make a mental note to keep your focus
without losing your cool.
Use your bench time as your game-time correction tool.

To stop look and learn from your
mistakes is good food for thought.
There is always a lesson learned and a lesson taught.

Encourage your teammates and give them support
As you project the image that you are a good sport.

Little things that count big

These are a few little things that
players may think don't matter.
If you give the extra effort, they can
help you move up on the ladder.

Always put the mustard zip and snap
when you make every pass.
Ensure you shoot every lay-up high up on the glass.

Don't get upset on offense or worried
when you make a mistake.
Just sprint back down the court to
defend against the fast break.

Constantly move without the ball and set a solid pick.
Whenever you make a cut or fake,
you should always make it quick.

Whenever a loose ball is on the floor,
be the first player to take a dive.
Play with the heart of a warrior and
you will always survive.

Whenever any shot goes up find a man to box-out
Then jump to get the rebound and always go all-out.

Hustle back on defense and always defend the lane.
Stop any player driving and be ready to absorb the pain.

Jump stop with your feet planted to draw the charge.
Stand wide and flex your body to make yourself large.

Make it a habit on defense to keep active
hands and stay light on your feet.
Put pressure on every ball handler that you meet.

Look him dead in the eyes and never show any fear.
Give him that game face look to let him
know he gets nothing easy here!

Walk and talk with this mentality
and wear it on your sleeve.
You can amaze yourself with good
defense if you only believe.

Basketball Greatness

What makes a player go from good to great?
It is staying focused with your head on straight.

It's a player with swagger and attitude,
arrogant yet always humble with gratitude.

Always play all out with hunger, heart and hustle.
It's using your head, with quickness and mental muscle.

What makes great players rise to the top
and distinguish themselves as the cream of the crop.

They work hard until they're about to drop
and even then they just don't stop!

They never blame the referees for bad
calls or the gym conditions,
tight rims, bad court surface, their
teammates or the game statisticians.

Winners play above the problems and
don't make excuses or alibis.
You can spot a winner a mile away by the
look of determination in their eyes.

Great players never let their opponent or
outside conditions control their game.
They know winning and losing comes down
to who can stay focused and tame.

They are mentally conditioned, cool,
calm and mentally tough.
They don't get frustrated under pressure
or when the going gets rough.

Winners don't dwell on past mistakes they
themselves or their teammates make.
They play harder, bounce back and counter
attack like it's a piece of cake.

Great players hate to lose more than they like to win.
Great players never give up thru thick and thin.

They still play hard whether their team is twenty
points down or has a twenty-point lead.
They play within their team concept
instead of selfish greed.

It's Not What You Say

At the end of the day, it's not what you say;
it's whether or not you came to play.
Let your game speak volumes for itself
is the best and positive way.

No need to trash talk, brag or boast.
True ballers talk less and say the most.

Do you want the ball for the game winning shot?
Do you always play with fire and desire;
are you always blazing hot?

Do you play with attitude, but always humble?
Can you lose with grace and not complain or grumble?

Do you have the killer instinct and
walk with the swagger?
Can you knock down the big shots under
pressure and deliver the dagger?

If you get knocked down 99 times,
do you still keep playing?
No matter what people in the stands are saying?

Can you stand the heat when the coach gets on your case?
Can you ignore a defender when he gets up in your face?

Can you deliver the shot as a knockout blow?
Can you play in control and in the flow?

If you make a mistake can you forgive and forget?
Like it's history, a mystery, and a counterfeit?

No Gym?

Can't get to a gym for whatever reason?
You can still improve your game no matter what season.

Try this basketball workout when you
can't get to a gym or court.
Use your imagination, relax and visualize
yourself excelling in this sport.

You can use the imaginary DVD
video player of your mind.
See yourself shooting baskets in a
video and repeatedly rewind.

Relax yourself physically and stay mentally tame.
A mind that is filled with stress cannot
play its best basketball game.

No matter how much stress you currently feel,
you can learn to relax and play with nerves of steel.

No matter how much of yesterday
you are carrying into today,
you can get yourself to emotionally deflate within
seconds and be ready to compete and play.

Basketball Visionetics can be applied
just before you go to sleep.
Simply visualize yourself shooting nothing
but swishes, just like counting sheep.

Over and over rehearsal in repetition,
over-night preparation for better competition.

See the sizzle, and watch the flame,
hear the nets rip as you win the game.

Feel that perfect release and shooting stroke,
automatic and deadly, it's not a joke.

With perfect arc, rotation and spiral,
spinning on target while becoming viral.

Practice defensive stance, get low, hands
up and out and ready to snatch.
Be ready to take away space from the player,
close the lane and take their catch.

Practice your handle dribbling the figure
eight, bending low with a tennis ball.
Do one and two foot calf raises with your hands up tall.

Practice the fall to get the charging, offensive foul call.
Get in a defensive stance squat for a 30 count
with your back leaning against a wall.

Repeat everything over and over in sets of ten.
Envision every shot taken going straight in.

Get in a squared stance and release the ball
quickly as you jump on the way up.

Don't watch the ball flight, just stare at an imaginary
crossbar + centered above the square at the cup.

Practice shooting your jumper without
the ball in front of a mirror.
With perfect form it doesn't get any clearer.

Rehearse the double crossover and then take the step back.
Head fake and explode as you lunge,
then drive to the rack.

One or two dribbles are all you really need to score.
Fake to the front, side, or spin-off and go back door.

Master the half spin, the behind the
back and the stutter step
Use fakes with attacking quickness and plenty of pep.

Jap step to the left, to the back or jab step to the right.
Always have the backboard and goal within your eyesight.

You can practice wherever you are.
Even when you are riding in a car.

Memorize jab steps, dribble moves and pump shot fakes.
Make the counter move based on the defenders mistakes.

Practice without the ball making the perfect pass.
Practice knocking down jumpers from
the wing that kiss the glass.

Practice shooting from these five spots on the floor.
Feet square, knees bent, shot pocket set
with your eyes ready to score.

The two corners, two wings and the top of the key.
Inside shots ten times around, then
ten times shoot the three.

Protect the ball with your body, use your weight.
Balance, Elbows in, Eyes up Follow thru straight.

Move away from any hand in your face.
Use jab steps, pivots and fakes to get your open space.

Fake up, step under, knock down the shot.
Fake up, step back and nail another from the same spot.

Fake up shot left, then pull the
trigger or drive to the right.
Fake up shot right, attack the left side
strong lay-up scoring in flight.

Use low crossovers stutter step, then give and go.
Cut hard to your spot to shoot on
the wing or inside and low.

Cross out in front, between the legs or behind your back.
Cross them up with the double moves and
the pressure will make them crack.

Keep your head up, use your shoulders
with the quickness of foot-speed.
Make your defender give you the scoring space you need.

Use your non-dribbling arm as a guard
to direct traffic and as a shield.
Dribble turn slightly cornered, make sure you
can always see the whole playing field.

I Am!

I am a great shooter!
I use perfect form and muscle
memory just like a computer.

I can score anywhere on the court.
I love this game! I love this sport!

I always shoot relaxed, cool, under
pressure yet calm and collected.
My shots are within the context of the game; never
forced or selfish and never blocked or rejected.

I am a winner and I know I've got game.
My shooting form is wholesome pure, it's
accurate and sure, it's always the same.

Every shot I take, I shoot to make. Sometimes I
give a good head and shoulder pump fake.
I can finish in traffic or on the fast break and
all my free throws are like a piece of cake!

You can count the money from the ATM.
My shots don't even touch the nets or rim.

I can shoot with a hand in my face
and I'll bust that jumper, I don't need
that much time or space.

I can shoot three's with ease
from all angles and degrees.

I can shoot the bank shot with the kiss.
I can get hot, hit the spot and never miss.

I get buckets from all over the court;
inside, outside, or the outside and in.
I hate to miss shots like it's a cardinal sin.
I hate to lose games more than I like to win.

I always bring my "A" game and play hard-core.
I do whatever it takes and always leave it on the floor.

You Shoot a Perfect Jump Shot!

Do you want to make every shot?
Or just wish it would go?
If you want to shoot like a pro, you
better act like you already know!

You can make it rain from any scoring spot.
Your shot is on fire and flaming, sizzling hot.

You always shoot with a picture perfect stroke.
You shoot with a quick release that is not a joke.

You shoot a perfect jump shot!

You shoot loaded darts like seasoned ninja sniper.
Your trigger finger snaps and stings just like a viper.

Your non-shooting hand is like a
sun visor to give you shade.
This form is automatic and custom tailor made.

Your shot splashes dead center so the nets don't move.
Your shot is calibrated with a magnetic groove.

Your shot smoothly swishes like automatic.
You always shoot with great rotational static.

You shoot a perfect jump shot!

Your shot spirals straight up and over the rim.
You can always get viral shooting any where in the gym.

Your feet are always well grounded
with a staggered stance.
It gives your body a better angle for better chance.

You shoot with the BEEF form on
balance and you get space.
You knock down shoots with hands in your face.

Elbows in and above your eye in the shooting socket.
Elevating with the down-up hop from a mini rocket.

You shoot a perfect jump shot!

Eyes focused on the center of the
white inner backboard square.
Envision the ball dropping from a chute
just a few inches above there.

Follow thru with focus, freeze and hold that pose.
It can also help you draw fouls, the
basket's good if it goes.
Put in the workout until your mind and body knows.

It will pay off in the long run if you use these steps.
Execute deep perfect practice with
hundreds of daily consistent reps.

Plant these powerful mental habitual seeds.
As mentioned before, the best practice every baller needs
is to take game-shots, from game spots at game speeds.

Shoot from the corners, elbows, and the wings
for the sure pureness to enjoy the benefit it brings.

You shoot a perfect jump shot!

Shot Repair

This next passage explains why you miss jump shots.
It also tells how to make corrections
and adjustments on the spot.

Shots are missed for one of these four reasons:
too long/too short or off to the left or right.
Here's how to re-align or adjust the basketball
release, the shooting arch and flight.

If the ball is too short, use more leg
power and upward force.
If the ball is too long then too much
power is the cause and source.

If the ball is bounces off the rim on the left or right side,
your non-shooting hand and elbow is not close to
your body; it's extended out too far and wide.

If a player's shot is falling short, they are not
using enough power from the legs and knees.
If the ball is hitting to the left or right of the basket,
the shooter is not keeping their elbow
straight and arm at ninety degrees.

It can also come from not holding the follow-thru
for a count of one thousand one, one thousand two.

If the ball is spinning out, the shooting hand
is not right behind the ball,
Sidespin is taking over which causes the
side-ways spiral of the ball as it falls.

Use muscle memory to make the
adjustment and correction.
Rehearse the right mechanics in your
mental pre-shot projection.

Observe your breathing to reveal if you are too tense,
whenever you shoot against good defense.

Inhale and exhale normally as let your breath flow,
simply relax and let your shot go.

Don't give your mind the time to think or calculate.
Take the sure and pure shot with
quickness, do not resist or hesitate.

Crunch Time!

When the game is on the line with no timeouts
left and ten seconds is all you've got,
Can you handle the pressure and knock down the shot?

Can you shoot the ball with a hand in your face?
Can you get your shot off even if you don't have space?

Can you knock down the shot and take physical contact?
When the ref doesn't call the foul, can you
make the shot in spite of that fact?

It doesn't matter if you are the home team or away.
Don't listen to crowd noise chatter, just relax and play.

Just be cool, calm, and collective;
there is no need to panic.
Just go thru your basic shooting mechanics.

Always know where you are on the court
and locate the back center of the rim.
This is your automatic concentration and
focus point in any basketball gym.

Shoot the ball quickly with a pure, sure release and stroke.
Shoot with the confidence like you "ain't a joke!"

Shoot like it is ordinary, simple, easy and plain.
Shoot with the hardwired muscle
memory from your brain.

Shoot squared up on balance with perfect form.
Shoot every shot as if it's the norm.

Shoot every shot with robotics with a fluid-like groove.
Shoot the rock straight up and over
the rim so the nets don't move.

Shoot like you've been there and done that before.
Shoot like you don't even care about the score.

Shoot confidently like you know you can win any game.
Shoot like you want to hear the crowd say your name.

Score the shot first in your mind as a sure shot dagger.
Splash the shot in crunch time with deliberate swagger.

Free Throw Ritual

Here's a free throw shooting ritual.
It's what players should make habitual.

Keep the same form and release every
time you shoot a free throw.
Step to the line with confidence and act like you know.

Make the shot in your mind before you even shoot.
See it, feel it, and hear the net swish to boot.

Take a staggered foot stance and bend at the knees.
Inhale then exhale, relax and just be at ease.

Stay focused on the goal and the
middle net ring of the rim.
Shoot the same shot release at every court and gym.

Keep every shot motion the same
and simple as one, two three.
Just knock down the shot because it's free!

Hold your follow through till the ball hits the floor.
Make sure the basket is counted to
add one point to the score.

Overcoming Losing

How do you handle losing? Do you love
to win? Do you hate defeat?
Do you point fingers at your teammates and
coach or swear the referees cheat?

Do you review the game in your mind
and accept any part of the blame?
Do you feel guilty for not playing your hardest?
Do you feel any remorse or shame?

If you could play the game over what
part would you change?
Would you make your all your foul shots and
lay-ups or shoot within your range?

Would you take the offensive charge
and play harder on defense?
Would you hustle every chance you could
no matter what the expense?

Would you take your opponent more seriously
instead of for taking them for granted?
Could you have ignored the crowd noises and
the trash talk they repeatedly chanted?

No matter what the cause, whether
there is rhyme or reason.
Reflect on the outcome and move on
to play the rest of the season.

Don't let it fester or simmer too long
in your mind and marinate.
Erase the negative feelings so it doesn't contaminate.

It is history, just one episode, and the end of a show.
Just move on to the next game,
forgive, forget and let it go.

No need to carry excess baggage and
let it weigh down your mind.
Get a good night's sleep and ask your subconscious
to seek ways to improve and you will find.

Ask yourself what went wrong and what went right?
Did you bring enough ammunition to
convincingly win the fight?

Did you do all you could to enable
your team to play their best?
Did you go to bed early the night
before and get enough rest?

If you could replay the game, if you had another chance,
would you step on the court with a more defensive stance?

Did you stick to the game plan and
did you stay on the course?
Was your strategy and tactics good or
did you need another source?

Your questions will be answered as you awaken
refreshed at the start of the next day.
You will be revived with positive energy,
enthusiasm and ready to play.

Mental Toughness

Mental toughness comes from within. It's
the mindset where champions begin.
Can you take a punch right on the chin? Can
you take the heat, do you have thick skin?

Do you hate to lose more than you like to win?
Do you hate to miss a shot like it's a cardinal sin?

Can you always play hard thru thick and thin?
Do you fall down, dust yourself off and get up again?

No need to trash talk, brag or boast.
True champions talk less but say the most.

Do you want the ball for the game winning shot?
Do you always play with fire and desire,
are you always inspired and hot?

Do you play with attitude, yet always humble?
Can you lose with grace and not complain,
whine or moan and grumble?

Are you combat ready and walk with the swagger?
Can you knock down shots under
pressure and deliver the dagger?

If you get knocked down 99 times,
do you still keep playing?
No matter what people in the stands are nay-saying?

Can you stand the heat when the coach gets on your case?
Can you ignore a defender when he gets up in your face?

Can you deliver the shot as a knockout blow?
Can you play in control and in the flow?

If you make a mistake can you forgive and forget,
like its history, a mystery, a counterfeit?

Do you want the ball in your hands
when the game is on the line?
Do you declare war and take over when
it's time to rise and shine?

All it takes is the mental mindset and frame!
You always play hard and you know you've got game.

Do you know how to take over the
game and set the pace and tone?
Do you know how to play smart in the competitive zone?

Do you have resiliency and always fight back?
Do you always hustle and never give any slack?

Can you defend or play at more than one position?
Do you play harder than your competition?

Do you move without the ball and always cut hard?
Do you make yourself a scoring threat
and always hard to guard?

Do you have basketball IQ and
understanding of the game?
Do you leave the scouts and coaches asking your name?

Are you consistent and reliable every
night in and night out?
Can your coach and team count on you down
the stretch without the benefit of a doubt?

Can you handle pressure and stay calm
no matter what the score?
Do you never give up playing and
always leave it on the floor?

Are You The Glue?

If your team was losing badly and about to fall apart,
could you come in as a sparkplug off the
bench to give them a jump-start?

Could you dig in deep and play with
all your heart and soul?
This is one of the requirements for you to play this role.

Can you hold your team together
when times are thick or thin?
Will you be the glue and do whatever it takes to win?

It's gritty, hardcore, scrappy nasty, and
sometimes down right dirty deeds.
It's the tooth and nail biting, scratching
that every good team needs.

Will you chase down 50/50 balls
and try to get deflections?
Can you change player's shots or get shot block rejections?

Can you be the unsung all star who doesn't get the credit?
Can you impact the game without the
glory and never even sweat it?

Will you help your team get focused if they
get rattled when times are tough?
Can you dig down deep within yourself to
fight and battle when it gets a little rough?

Will you sacrifice your body to take a defensive charge?
Can you be a pesky defender who makes
stops that come up large?

Will you play like a maniac even if
you don't get playing time?
Will you run the down the floor like
you just committed a crime?

Can you move without the ball to set
mean, lean and legal solid screens?
Can you do the unsung hero work that
goes unnoticed behind the scenes?

Will you play without thinking about
how many points you score?
Can you be the glue for your squad
who leaves it on the floor?

These are the intangible ingredients
in the recipe for the glue.
Now that you know this secret potion,
what are you going to do?

It Ain't the Shoes!

It ain't the socks, it ain't the shirt. It ain't
the sleeve, it "ain't" the shoes.
There's no secret sauce or magic formula that you can use.

Shoes won't make you a better baller.
Shoes won't help to play any taller.

Don't believe the media hoopla hysteria and hype.
It ain't the swoosh, a star or the triple stripe.

$250 shoes don't make a player into a superstar,
It's a sneaker pipe dream that won't take you very far.

Shoes won't help you to slam-dunk.
It's an urban legend that is full of bunk.

There's nothing worse than player
who believes they have game,
as a by-product of the shoes they
rock with a famous name.

They don't pack your game inside of the box.
It doesn't come by default when you
wear a designer pair of sox.

You won't get your "A-game" from a
sleeve or a matching wristband.
It only comes from within if you truly understand.

Hard work beats talent when talent fails to work hard.
He who wins games put in the gym
time and went the extra yard.

It is the gym rat tolling away and doesn't
care where the next party is at.
The baller who puts in the grunt work to get
his jump shot and handle down pat.

The kind of baller who may only have
one pair of shoes.
The type who never met a basketball
challenge they couldn't refuse.

They play to better their game by any necessary means.
It oozes in their blood and is ingrained
in their DNA genes.

Bonafide ballers, certified and qualified on the court.
They played their hearts out for the undying
and undeniable love of the sport.

They wear the invisible tattoo of a baller with swagger.
Born to ball against all with the killer
instinct to knock down the dagger.

You can take away all their accessories but you can't deny.
They know they have a game that money cannot buy.

Teamwork

Teamwork is the key to a championship season.
Without it there is no rhyme or reason.

It's as easy as one, two, three.
Share the basketball with chemistry.

Always look to make the extra pass.
Be selfless and unselfish, it shows you have class.

Reward your big men battling in the paint
or for any type of hustle 50/50 play.
With a well-served, on target, in-stride
bounce pass, special delivery on a tray.

Always look up the floor for your teammates to score.
Cutting and moving at all times and
especially for the back door.

Keep everybody happy is the key to win.
It only comes when everybody plays
united as one team from within.

You always play with laser-like focus and concentration.
You defend with tenacity, intimidation and determination.

You play the game with mental motivation,
precision, intensity and teamwork assistance.

You always shoot with a consistent release
and stroke with persistence.
Always maintain the defensive vice-like lockdown grips.
Offense wins fans but defense wins championships.

If you take a close look at championship games and
took a closer statistic review and inspection.
The winning team usually had the most rebounds,
steals or deflections, 50/50 balls and shot rejections.

The players reigned havoc and tenacity.
Defense on steroids is a mindset that has to be.

Attack the offense with hands like swordsman out to slay.
Swipe the ball up, out and away,
swarming pest-like tough tenacious defense,
is the way you must always play.

It starts with the point guard who plays like a traffic cop.
He directs the ball handler to one side from the top.

The wings must then step in and jump to the ball.
They must keep the pressure to drive
the ball handler into a wall.

The forwards protect the paint and
keep players out of the lane.
They punish any trespassers and make them feel the pain.

All five players work together like fingers in a glove.
Teamwork to the tenth power of basketball love.

Talking non-stop and always helping
when ever there is a need.
Watching every movement with a
hawk-eye alertness and read.

Always moving active hands and active feet,
with heads on a swivel make a defense complete.

Stay

Thirsty
Hungry
Hungry
Honorable
Game Face Ready
Cool, Calm, Collective
Chill and always steady
Stay focused, stay disciplined
Stay aggressive
Stay tough
Stay tenacious
Stay basketball possessive
Stay relentless
Stay fearless
Stay bold
Stay nasty, feisty and scrappy
Stay confident, Stay courageous
Stay positive, confident,
Stay hustling, alert, active with your hands
and quickly step slide your feet.
Moving without the ball
Cut hard, cut sharp, cut deliberate and quick
Keep cutting and moving, make your defender sick
Cut to the box, spin-off and sprint to the wing
Cut to the wing and go back door
Use your slickness and quickness to get open and score

Basketball Swagger

Bring your basketball swagger whenever
you step on the court to play.
With a defensive snarl on your face that says
"Go ahead, and try to make my day.

Wear a riddler's smile like a card-
shark with a winning hand.
Play every possession like it's worth one hundred grand.

Protect the ball on offense and
Protect the paint when you defend.

Play with a do or die attitude,
Even against your best friend.

Take no prisoners, and don't give any slack.
Always have your teammates back.

Be aggressive, deliberate and play with passion.
Show no fear in any form or fashion.

Hit the floor with determination and desire.
Hustle like your pants just caught on fire.

Play with purpose, that's how you run and how you roll.
Play with your head, your heart and soul

Swagger can't be faked; it has to be real.
Swagger comes from within; it's how you feel.

It's a secret potion, a secret sauce.
It let's everybody know that you are the boss.

You don't have to announce or put yourself on blast.
Swagger is a signal that will self broadcast.

You know you have swagger when you get respect.
You are confident when you have the swagger effect.

Swagger can't be brought in stores or on the internet.
Swagger can only be earned gym time
hours of hard work, blood and sweat.

Hoop Soup for the Baller's Soul

There's nothing more powerful than a healthy bowl
of wholesome Hoop Soup for the basketball
player's mind, body and soul.

Here's the secret scientific and holistic recipe
for better basketball mental chemistry.

Start with five wholesome deep breaths of air.
Focus on the backboard and rim with a constant stare.

Stir slowly and carefully with your power
of game playing visualization.
Sprinkle in a mixture of creativity and improvisation.

Let these thoughts simmer for five minutes and marinate,
while you strategize like a chess master and calculate.

Prepare to play with a ton of heart, fueled
with unlimited doses of tireless energy.
Add the mixture of the synchronicity and synergy.

Use your skills and always play with basketball IQ.
So you will always know what to do.

Keep this potion in a bottle mentally sip and drink,
eat, sleep and basketball think!

Devour as much as you like till it drips like sweat
that oozes from your pores and bones.
It's the hoop soup to cure any ailment or basketball Jones!

How Bad Do You Want It?

Will you push yourself to the edge
and beyond the extreme?
Do you also strive to push and lead your team?

Do you want it so bad you can see it in your mind?
If you seek and search hard enough, then you shall find.

Will you stay on point when the road gets tough?
Will you stick with the game plan even when it's rough?

If you want it so bad, will you do whatever it takes?
Will you correct yourself when you make mistakes?

Will you train on your own without being told?
Will you go no matter the weather hot or cold?

Will you mentally practice and visualize in your mind?
Do you look for all the training you can find?

Will you practice taking and making
hundreds of imaginary shots,
around the court from the top seven scoring spots.

Can you keep going even when the haters hate?
Did you know that good things come
to those train and never wait?

Do you practice with purpose and a master plan?
Do you challenge yourself to be better
than you think you can?

If you do this homework each and every day,
within two months, you should notice
improvement in how you play.

If you want to get better and even further excel,
then keep doing these exercises and you will do well.

How bad do you want it? How hard will you try?
Do you know your reason for playing; your reason why?

That reason is your purpose. It's your carrot on the stick.
It's the method to your madness and what makes you tick.

It's the spark and catalyst that starts the flame burning
and gives you fuel and the quest to keep on yearning.

Wear that passion of fire and desire
like a tattoo on your sleeve.
You will amaze yourself when you accomplish
what you will believe and achieve.

Wanted: A Junkyard Dog

This player must know the meaning of scrap,
He will hit the floor before your fingers can snap.

Coaches love a junk yard dog part Rottweiler, part Pit,
pedigree that continues to get stronger
when fighting and will never quit.

You won't see him smile, instead he wears a mean scowl,
He's known for his bark and bite on
the court with menacing growl

He crashes the board on each and every shot,
Boxing out his man to the perfect rebounding spot.

He brings the pressure with active hands and feet.
He fights to the finish and will never retreat.

He will help defend and protect the lane
He will drive any opponent insane.

He plays relentlessly with wreckless abandon.
He will fight for loose balls and be the last man standing.

He will box out any rebounder like his life is on the line.
He will never back down, give up or moan and whine.

He loves to win, but hates even more to lose.
He's the kind of player coaches love to choose.

His passion, hustle, humbleness, hunger and heart,
Make him a diamond in the rough, a true work of art.

He is all over the court and never tires.
He never stops playing until the clock expires.

He isn't concerned with points or other selfish statistics.
He does the dirty work and the
behind the scenes logistics.

He doesn't care about trophies, honors or awards,
He's the player who thrives and thirsts
on crashing the boards.

He will sacrifice his body and do whatever it takes.
His unselfish and relentless play results in lucky breaks.

Always playing with a sense of urgency,
running everywhere on the court like
a paramedic on an emergency.

He will always bring his game grime and grit,
His blood, sweat, scrapiness, polish and spit.

He will always leave his imprint and
impact no matter what the score.
He will let it shine and glisten as he
leaves it all on the floor.

Always!

Always play hard, always play smart, always play together,
Winning or losing, through thick and
thin or any type of weather.

The will to prepare is more important
than the will to win,
Perfection in practice is where championship runs begin.

Play solid basketball possession by possession,
Take care of the ball and make it an obsession.

Protect the rock and always handle
like fine china with care.
Secure it like a precious diamond that is rare.

Teamwork means surrender the individual
me for the collective we.
Play with team help defense and chemistry.

Every player can be big on the little
but important and vital things.
They help your team win championship rings.

Little things like boxing out on every shot.
Like beating the offense to the ball or the spot.

Then taking the charge with both feet planted.
Little things that players often take for granted.

Four quarters all for one and one for all.
That's the way to play winning basketball.

Offense wins fans, the glitter, the
hype, the bling and the glory,
Defense wins championships, the unsung hero,
and now you know the rest of the story.

Be ye ever ready, willing and able to defend,
from the beginning in the middle right up until the end.

Contest every shot and always close out without a doubt.
Keep both hands up, no need to jump,
and always block your man out.

Jump to the pass, pressure and trace the ball.
Make yourself big while you make your defender small.

This is a war so be ever ready to hit the floor!
Play with all out intensity no matter what the score.

Always try to outrun your opponent on the fast breaks.
Keep moving without the ball, do whatever it takes.

Beast-Play

Unleash the beast from within your mental cage.
Let yourself go and play with a beast-like rage.

Do you have the eyes of a tiger whenever you play?
Is your heart like a lion each and every day?

Will you bring your "animal" game upon your arrival,
playing like a predator; the last man standing in survival?

Can you roam the court like a raging bear?
Will you play aggressive defense with a panther-like stare?

Can you scrap in the lane like a bull in a china shop.
Boxing out anyone in your path and you just don't stop?

Will you play every game scene like a wolverine?
Will you always play hungry, lean and mean?

Can you hit the boards like a swooping condor?
Will you run the floor like a stampeding boar?

With or without the ball are you elusive
like a lizard and hard to guard?
Do you take advantage of court floor
space; every inch and every yard?

Do you make leopard-like quick moves, cuts and fakes?
Can you make up ground for
turnovers and your mistakes?

Are you unpredictable like a fox and hard to check?
Do you keep the other team frustrated and
annoyed like a pain in the neck?

Are you always in a good cat-like stance
in the right place and time?
Do you have quick, slick pickpocket hands
on the ball like it should be a crime?

Can you play like a coiled cobra and
stealthy ninja assassin?
Will you go all out like a raging rhino
with deliberate fashion?

Do you adapt like a chameleon to the flow
of the game and channel your energy?
Can you play unselfish team ball to build team synergy?

These are few of the beast mode
things that coaches look for:
habits of heart, hustle, and survival
mentality, no matter what the score.

Bibliography and other basketball resources for better playing

Stuff Good Players Should Know by Dick Devenzio

Stronger Team.com by Alan Stein (Strength and Conditioning Coach for Dematha High School)

Toughness by Jay Bilas

Tennis – Play the Mental Game and be in the zone every time you play by David Ranney www.maxtennis.com

Psycho-cybernetics by Matt Fuery

The Little Book of Afformations by Noah St. Johns

Sports Hypnosis

The Art of War by Sun Tzu

Mind Power in the 21st Century by John Kehoe

Tune Your Brain – Using Music to Manage Your Mind, Body and Mood by Elizabeth Miles

Superlearning 2000 by Sheila Ostrander and Lynn Ostrander

Self-Hypnosis The Key to Athletic Success by John G. Kappas, PhD

Unlimited Power - A Black Choice by Anthony Robbins & Joseph McClendon III

Acknowledgments

To Almighty God, maker of heaven and earth, who created and loves us all.
You enabled me to experience so much in life through the game of basketball.

To Gale my loving and beautiful wife, for your belief in my ability and untiring support during my long hours of research and writing.

To my mother Rev. Dora L. Atlas – my strength, role model, a modern-day miracle worker, you've paved the way; demonstrating the power of prayer, faith, charity, humility and forgiveness. Believe it or not, your Cub Scout Den mother principles influenced my coaching style.

To my father, the late Albert L. Atlas - whose hard and enduring work ethic ensured my sister, brother and I graduated from college. Departing too soon, yet you've been with me in spirit. Your shoulders carried me when I thought I did have the strength. Your acts of charity and selfless sacrifice and dedication to the church and community service were my inspiration and motivation.

My sister Jean –your encouragement gave me the permission to succeed, taught me class, music appreciation. When you took me to see Al Williams and Julius Erving play Hempstead against Roosevelt, Long Island, NY high school games, it ignited a fire in me for the love of the game.

Paul Atlas - my brother; your music is incredibly harmonious.

Our one on one basketball battles gave us the mettle to keep playing even after we got cut.

Lennitt Bligen, my brother – You broke the game down to me! I learned from you and it set me free.

Julius Erving – ambassador of the sport, we idolized you on and off the court.

Sandra Jamison –my cousin; you told me I could do it! Thanks for your most valuable research and assistance.

Lawrence Jackson - childhood friend, who encouraged me to coach his daughter's team at Morningside Elementary School, Morningside, MD, my partner with Hoop Mountain and Mid Atlantic Select AAU

Billy Holt (RIP) – the legendary baller from Hempstead, NY; my point guard, a great friend and coach.

Brad Harvey - my closest friend like a brother, we used to battle in the paint and punish players who dared to play against us at Campbell Park, Hempstead, NY.

Billy and Dennis Burgess - who mentored me at Campbell Park.

Ricky Cooke – childhood friend, nicknamed Hi-C because he jumped so high. Thanks for all you've done to urge the Hempstead youth to "carry the books as well as the ball".

To the legion of Hempstead ball players; too many to mention, who have impacted me in some shape, form or fashion. We played the game with deliberate spirited and tenacious passion. We are a basketball family.

Don Ryan – one Soldier of a Coach, with over 50 years community service, a tireless laborer and still impacting Hempstead basketball.

Sergeant Major (retired) Marshall Williams - thanks for letting me coach your son Maurice (Mo'), now a point guard at West Point.

To my coaching buddy and friend Wesley Broddie: thanks for partnering with me to coach Atlas-Hoops AAU and giving me the opportunity to work with your son Randall. I've watched him grow, mature and along the way witnessed him do amazing things on the court. I can't wait to see him in college. Your mental toughness approach and strategic planning enabled us to develop a coaching synergy that produced successful winning teams from 2008-2013.

To my good friend and fellow US Army soldier, Lionel Roberson, NBA Hoop It Up DC Championship teammate in 2003 and Joint Staff Bulls squad at the Pentagon: Thanks for inviting your god-son, the high flying, gravity defying, Charles Shedrick (now playing at Clayton State University) to the Hoop Mountain Exposure Camp in 2009. Our mastermind discussions on how to motivate him and other players has also influenced aspects of my writing.

About the Author

Coach Edwin L. Atlas brings 40+ years playing and coaching experience at the high school, AAU, Boys & Girls Club, YMCA and youth recreational levels. Coach Atlas personally witnessed highlight moves of ABA/ NBA All Star Julius Erving as a youth and played on the same playgrounds in his hometown of Hempstead, Long Island, NY. His journeyed tour of basketball began in 1970 as a sophomore at Palmer Memorial Institute in Sedalia, NC, where he played one season of junior varsity ball. He returned to Hempstead NY for his junior and senior years but failed to make the highly competitive Hempstead High School team. This inspired him to coach his younger brother Paul at the age of 17. Coach Atlas attended Livingstone College in Salisbury, NC and after unsuccessful walk-on tryout, he again coached his brother's YMCA team. Thus an early coaching career began to take shape. Despite being cut from the college team he played intramural basketball and continued to work on his game. He coached several high school level summer league teams in Hempstead, NY and Livingstone College's Upward Bound Youth team. After graduation from Livingstone College, Coach Atlas played a season in Randolph County, NC industrial league composed of local former college players. In 1979 enlisted in the US Army, where he played with competitive basketball for military teams with the US Army for twenty three (23) years, including a semi-professional season in Istanbul, Turkey concurrent with his military tour. His globe-trotting experience spans playing and coaching stints in South Korea, Turkey and Italy, in addition to several states including DC, MD, VA, IN, NC, SC, TX, and OK. He played for several White House and Pentagon basketball teams during his military career. Upon retirement from the US Army in 2002 Coach Atlas devoted ten years coaching youth in the Silver Hill Boys and Girls Club teams, Temple Hills, MD. Coach Atlas assisted with St. Charles Elementary School, Alexandria, VA and Morningside Elementary School, Camp Springs, MD teams. He also coached with the MD Blazers, Mid Atlantic Select and Atlas Hoops AAU programs. His dedication and devotion to basketball development has manifested in the number of former players currently playing high school and college basketball. Coach Atlas was Director of Player Personnel for Hoop Mountain Mid Atlantic Boys College Exposure clinics for one season. Additionally he was as assistant freshman coach with St. John's College HS, Washington, DC for the 2012 season. His love for the game and impacting youth continues to motivate him to stay involved in the game through personal coaching, consulting and mentorship. This extensive basketball biography enabled, empowered and inspired Coach Atlas to compose the contents of Basketball Visionetics. He can be reached for consultation and personal coaching by e-mail at: gameface@atlas-hoops.com

If you're a basketball player who wants to know the secrets of basketball, mental preparation, then you're about to discover how to play your best basketball right now!

In fact, if you want to know how to play better basketball every game, then this new book - "Basketball Visionetics: Mental Preparation for Better Play" - gives you the answers to four important questions and challenges every basketball players faces, including:

- How can you get mentally prepared to play better basketball?
- Does mental preparation help basketball players play better
- How can you use affirmations to help basketball players?

What to do when you play badly or lose games… and more!

So, if you're serious about wanting better basketball play and you want to know how to play better basketball every game, then you need to grab a copy of "Basketball Visionetics: Mental Preparation for Better Play" right now, because basketball expert, Edwin Atlas, will reveal to you how every basketball player, regardless of experience level, can succeed - Today!